To order additional copies of this book, contact:
Xlibris
844-714-8691
www.Xlibris.com
Orders@Xlibris.com

ISBN: 978-1-6641-9183-9 (sc)
ISBN: 978-1-6641-9185-3 (e)

Print information available on the last page

Rev. date: 11/09/2021

I would like to dedicate this book
to my granddaughters, Shakevia,
who's afraid of anything that
creeps, crawls or flies and
to Cloey, who's fearless.

I would like to thank my sister,
Mary Martin, for encouraging
me to write this book.

I'm afraid of sitting
on the ground,

because I know there
are bugs around.

I'm afraid of flies
that fly around,

little ants on
the ground.

I'm afraid of
butterflies that
spread their wings,

little birds that
chirp and sing.

I'm afraid of
mosquitoes that buzz
around my ears.

They nearly drive
me to tears.

I'm afraid of red and black ladybugs,

Wiggly worms and slimy slugs.

I'm afraid of playing around the fruit trees,

Because there are so many bumble bees.

I'm afraid of spending
time at the lake,

Because of the fear
of seeing a snake.

I'm afraid of
spiders and any
insect that flies,

They make me want
to cover my eyes.

I'm afraid of anything
that creeps or crawls,

Please, please get
rid of them all.

I don't want them
around me.

I'll just stay inside
and watch T.V.

Printed in the United States
by Baker & Taylor Publisher Services